Wealthy Lotus

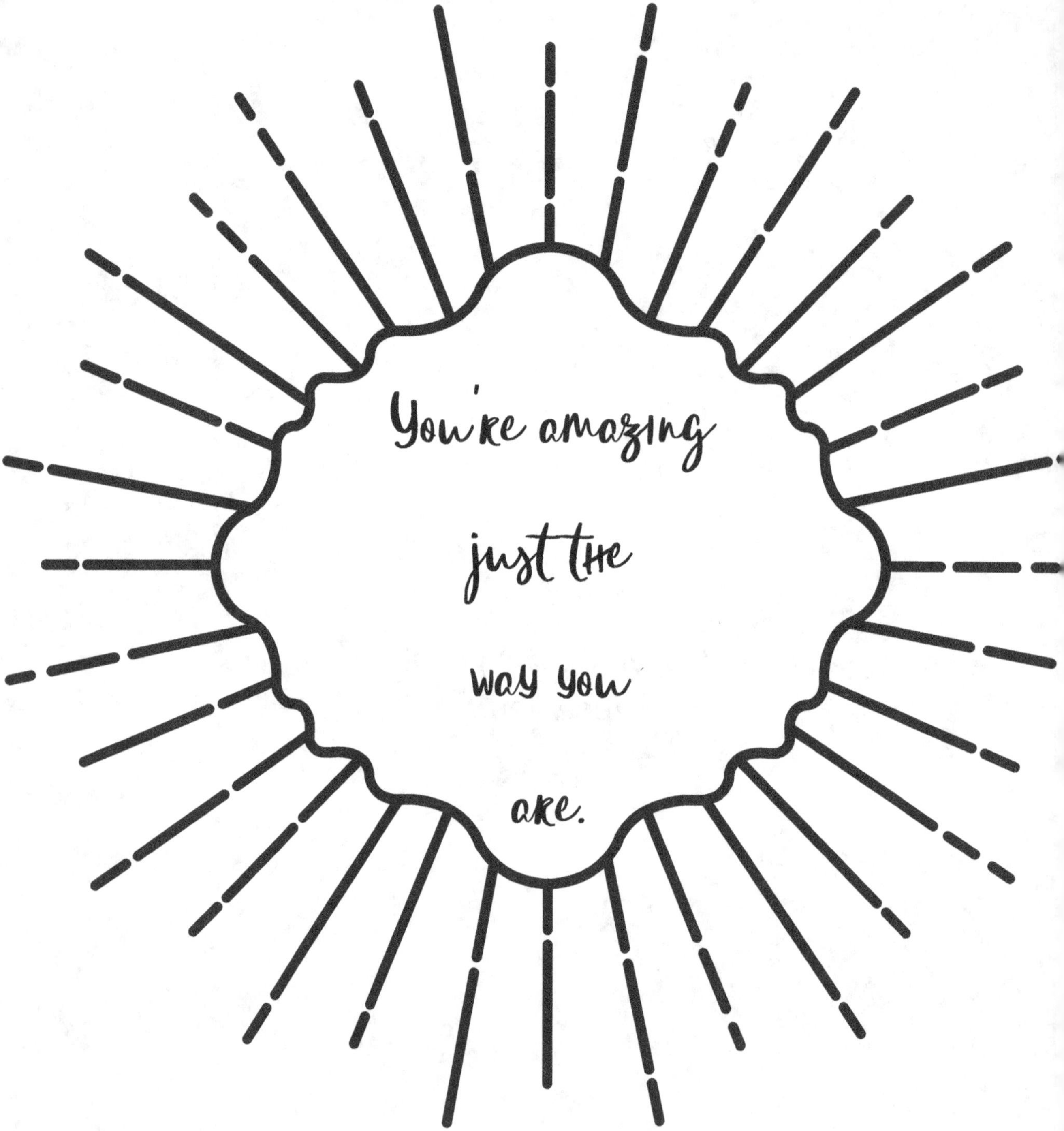
You're amazing
just the
way you
are.

www.ingramcontent.com/pod-product-compliance
Lightning Source LLC
Chambersburg PA
CBHW081730220526
45468CB00008B/2043
* 9 7 8 1 7 2 3 9 6 6 9 8 9 *